"My—my pin!" Tora cried, pointing at Fabio as he flew away. "That thing took the only part of the city I had left!"

Isla could hear Fabio's new, awful song ringing through the market. *"It's mine! It's mine! So shiny and divine! Poor wingless creatures, you'll never catch me!"*

Quickly, Isla grabbed her helmet and picked up her bike. "I know where he lives. You don't have to come if you don't want to. I wouldn't want you to get your bike dirty."

Until Fabio showed up for his solo.

"Well, well, well!" the bird called as he circled in the sky. "If it isn't Isla and Frank!"

"Fitz! The name's Fitz!" Fitz shouted.

"Same thing!" Fabio said grandly. "Oh, and what do we have here? A gift? For *me*?"

What came next came fast, as adventures on the island can do.

Fabio saw the glint of Tora's pin, then swooped right in to snatch it!

"Don't worry about my bike," Tora said, in a sudden gust of bravery. "Let's get that bird!"

up and checked her vest pockets. She had her notebook, a pencil, and a few color markers. She was always ready for a little creative moment.

And in Sol, just about everything was inspiring.

"It smells delicious in here," said a familiar kind voice. "I should have come earlier!"

"ABUELO!" said Isla as she ran to her grandpa and hugged him tightly.

"Good morning, *chicas*!" said Abuelo. "And Fitz, of course."

Fitz sat on Isla's empty plate with a hand on his very full belly. "I need a minute. So full . . . of pancakes."

Abuelo wasn't like other grandpas.

He was a nature scientist, and today he was dressed for field work. He wore rolled-up pants, a vest with lots of pockets, a bucket hat, and old boots. And he never left home without his compass and binoculars.

Isla pointed to her own outfit. "We're matching!"

Abuelo let out a deep laugh. "*Perfecto!* Let's get going, then. I'll help your mama with snacks. Why don't you and Fitz wait by the car and think about what music we should play?"

Isla scooped up Fitz, kissed Mama goodbye, and headed outside.